DISCARD

CELEBRATING U.S. HOLIDAYS

Why Do We Celebrate
COLUMBUS DAY?

Darnell Petersen

PowerKiDS press.

New York

Published in 2019 by The Rosen Publishing Group, Inc.
29 East 21st Street, New York, NY 10010

First Edition

Editor: Brianna Battista
Book Design: Reann Nye

Photo Credits: Cover Joseph Reid/Alamy Stock Photos; p. 5 https://commons.wikimedia.org/wiki/File:Portrait_of_a_Man,_Said_to_be_Christopher_Columbus.jpg; p. 6, 24 Cvijovic Zarko/Shutterstock.com; p. 9 Charles Phelps Cushing/ClassicStock/Getty Images; pp. 10, 24 (ship) Bettmann/Getty Images; p. 13 Dioscoro Teofilo de la Puebla Tolin/Getty Images; pp. 14, 18 (Native People) Courtesy of the Library of Congress; p. 17 https://en.wikipedia.org/wiki/File:Landing_of_Columbus_(2).jpg; p. 21 dade72/Shutterstock.com; p. 22 Andy Katz/Pacifc Press/LightRocket/Getty Images; p. 24 Ievgenii Neyer/Shutterstock.com.

Cataloging-in-Publication Data

Names: Petersen, Darnell, author.
Title: Why do we celebrate Columbus Day? / Darnell Petersen.
Description: New York : PowerKids Press, 2019. | Series: Celebrating U.S. Holidays | Includes index.
Identifiers: LCCN 2017050218| ISBN 9781508166399 (library bound) | ISBN 9781508166412 (pbk.) | ISBN 9781508166429 (6 pack)
Subjects: LCSH: Columbus Day–Juvenile literature. | Columbus, Christopher–Juvenile literature. | America–Discovery and exploration–Spanish–Juvenile literature.
Classification: LCC E120 .P48 2019 | DDC 394.264–dc23
LC record available at https://lccn.loc.gov/2017050218

Manufactured in the United States of America

CPSIA Compliance Information: Batch #CS18PK: For Further Information contact Rosen Publishing, New York, New York at 1-800-237-9932

CONTENTS

Christopher Columbus was an explorer from **Italy**. He was born around 1451.

Europe

Spain

Asia

China

6

Columbus wanted to find a safer and quicker way to get to China.

Queen Isabella and King Ferdinand of Spain gave Columbus money for his trip.

8

Columbus set sail on August 3, 1492. His three **ships** were called the *Niña*, the *Pinta*, and the *Santa María*.

Columbus saw land on October 12, 1492. He called the people he met Indians.

People say Columbus "discoved the New World." However, Native Americans had been living there for thousands of years.

Many Europeans moved
to the Americas after
Columbus returned.

17

18

Columbus brought new goods and animals to the Americas. He brought horses, pigs, **wheat**, and sugar.

The United States would be very different if Columbus had not discovered the Americas by accident!

Many people celebrate Columbus Day with a day off from work and school. They celebrate Columbus as a great explorer.

Words to Know

Italy

ship

wheat

Index

Websites

Due to the changing nature of Internet links, PowerKids Press has developed an online list of websites related to the subject of this book. This site is updated regularly. Please use this link to access the list: www.powerkidslinks.com/ushol/colum